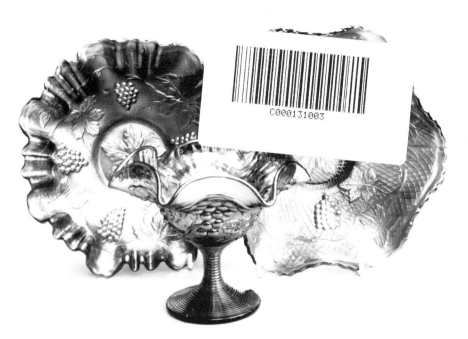

ABOVE: *Grape designs. The two bowls, by Fenton, are Vintage and Concord. The comport in the centre is made from a goblet in Imperial Grape design.*
COVER: *(From left to right: back) Beaded Bullseye vase (Imperial), Stag and Holly bowl (Fenton), Orange Tree hatpin holder (Fenton). (Centre) Leaf and Beads bowl (Northwood), Acorn Burrs tumbler (Northwood) in a Mayan bowl (Millersburg), and a peach-opalescent Question Marks comport (Dugan). At the front are a red, footed Panther bowl (Fenton) and an electric blue Holly and Berry bowl (Dugan) with serving handle.*

CARNIVAL GLASS

Raymond Notley

Shire Publications Ltd

CONTENTS

Published in 1995 by Shire Publications Ltd, Cromwell House, Church Street, Princes Risborough, Buckinghamshire HP27 9AA, UK. Copyright © 1983 and 1990 by Raymond Notley. First published 1983. Second edition 1986. Third edition 1990, reprinted with amendments 1995. Shire Album 104. ISBN 0 7478 0098 7.

Printed in Great Britain by CIT Printing Services, Press Buildings, Merlins Bridge, Haverfordwest, Dyfed SA61 1XF.

British Library Cataloguing in Publication Data: Notley, Raymond. Carnival glass. Third edition. 1. Carnival glassware, history. I. Title 748.29. ISBN 0-7478-0098-7.

ACKNOWLEDGEMENTS
All the glass illustrated was selected from the Notley-Lerpiniere Collection. It was photographed by the author. In the captions to the photographs the items illustrated are described from left to right, except where otherwise indicated. The author is grateful to the late William Heacock for the Butler Brothers advertisement shown on page 25.

All prime Carnival was made on hand-operated presses similar to this one.

P. SMITH & CO.,

MANUFACTURERS OF

Molds AND Machinery

FOR GLASS WORKS.

NO. 129 FIRST AVENUE,

NEAR WOOD STREET,

PITTSBURGH, PA.

P. SMITH.
W. S. McKEE.

Art Carnival. This graceful and wonderfully lustrous handled dish was shaped in the Northwood factory from a punch cup in the Grape and Cable pattern. A splendid and desirable object, it was sold originally for a few pennies.

INTRODUCTION

Ancient glass, in classic shapes and lustrous from burial, was much admired and copied in Europe during the last quarter of the nineteenth century. Using the antique and replica iridescent glass as a point of departure, Louis Comfort Tiffany and others in the United States produced new fluid shapes and textures. The chemistry of reproducing shimmering rainbow, golden and peacock hues and fixing them on glass was the subject of countless late Victorian patents. Glass technology had come into being. Fumes, vapours and exudations from heated metallic compounds were persuaded to stay as a thin surface film on vitreous material. Lustred pottery used the same process. The light interference patterns produced are within man's range of colour vision and the constantly shifting wavelengths are seen as a pleasing iridescence. A spray of stannous chloride is used to fix this thin layer. The noted glassmaker Frederick Carder confirmed that without this cheap spray neither his *Aurene* nor any other lustred glass would have been a success.

By 1886 the processes were so well known that Tiffany failed to obtain a patent for iridising glass and was allowed one only for an improvement on already well known methods. He was a dilettante genius and his exquisite and boldly overpriced iridescent glass started a trend which foreign factories soon catered for at lower prices. Iridescent flower tubes, from Bohemia, were offered for the Christmas trade of 1888 at prices, dependent on size, of between 2 and 18 shillings per dozen wholesale. Similar low prices were placed on Bohemian iridised goods when they reached the USA.

The first recorded mention of press-moulded glass with an iridescent finish is eight years before Tiffany's patent refusal. The *Pottery Gazette* in 1880 mentions

3

that Greener of Sunderland had pressed goods 'in all the usual nic-nacs' with an iridescent finish. Production must have been small for it is still not known what these 'nic-nacs' were. The notion of lustrous pressed glass is there but it was not perfected until later. However, expensive iridescent glass was still being made in the early twentieth century.

The Steuben works under Carder made *Aurene* glass, containing no gold but looking so like the Tiffany product that there were disputes and a lawsuit that was abandoned. The problem was the ease with which the actual iridescent surface could be copied. Carder summed the situation up in a sentence: 'When the maid could possess iridescent glass as well as her mistress, the latter promptly lost interest in it.'

The mass production of press-moulded glass with iridescence was inevitable. The lineage of Carnival is the same as that of all other intentionally iridised glass. It was, originally, a mass-produced art glass. It has the same cheap sprayed-on coating as its more expensive relatives.

LEFT: *Flower vases in contrasting style. Beaded Bullseye (Imperial), Daisy and Plume (Northwood) and Plumed Panel (Fenton). These cost 9d each when new.*

RIGHT: *Hatpin holder in Grape and Cable (Northwood). The three hatpins shown have their steel shanks inside the holder. The two at the front are Scarab and Rooster, with a geometric design behind. The origin of these pins is Bohemian.*

4

Catalogues of the Finnish Karhula-Iitala and Riihimäen Lasi Oy works show respectively the sugar bowl and creamer in the Diamond Ovals design and the Drapery Variant tumbler. It is interesting that the pitcher to match the tumbler is depicted in an Argentinian catalogue.

CLASSIFICATION OF CARNIVAL GLASS

This glass, when first made, was never known by or sold under the disparaging name of Carnival given to it in the 1950s. The name was a generic one applied to any obviously moulded glassware with an iridescent finish and arose because some secondary Carnival (though very little of the prime product) was offered at funfairs as prizes.

Carnival has been made in many countries, under many fanciful names and in several distinct periods since 1908. The top quality, or prime Carnival glass, was made in the United States, in or around the Ohio valley, between 1908 and 1918 Production was at its greatest between 1911 and 1925. This American-made prime glass is the most important type and forms the majority of extant examples of Carnival glass. Prime Carnival was very successful both on the domestic American market and as an export. Home interest waned, however, during the late 1920s but residual stocks enabled the makers to fulfil buoyant overseas orders. The last batches, from warehouse clearances, were shipped in 1930.

Secondary Carnival, of variable quality, still hand-pressed but with little manual finishing, was made in Australia during the 1920s, in Europe from around 1926 to 1939 and in Argentina during the 1930s. Many European moulds made their way to South America and others were copied there. It was marketed originally to rival the prime product but then was to replace it as American production ceased. Demand fell in Europe, and elsewhere, a few years after it had done in the USA. Production during the 1930s was sparse and spasmodic.

New Carnival, generally made from new moulds of new designs, appeared in the USA from the mid 1960s onwards, as did reproduction wares made in the old moulds. New and reproduction glass was a direct result of the systematic and organised collecting of prime Carnival in the United States.

There is also commercial and industrial Carnival in the form of bottles, insulators and other utilitarian artefacts that have been given an iridescent spray. Some *machine*-pressed pattern goods from moulds first used in the 1930s were reissued with an iridescent coating in the 1960s. All are part of the iridescent glass family. It is a matter of opinion as to how much should be classified as Carnival glass.

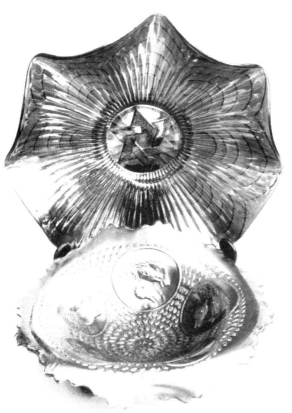

TOP LEFT: *Scroll Embossed shallow bowl (Imperial) with sawtooth edge, as moulded. It can be seen how easily such dishes were pushed down into the flat plate as shown.*

TOP RIGHT: *The delicate tripod open-edged bowl was pressed with a horizontal edge. The example shown has the edging pushed up. The design is Wild Rose (Northwood) and behind it is a Wild Blackberry bowl (Fenton) with the characteristic Fenton crimping known as Candy Ribbon.*

LEFT: *The Horses' Heads footed bowl (Fenton) in the foreground is pulled down at the front and tipped up at the back in a parody of the art glass 'Jack-in-the-Pulpit' shape. The Star of David bowl (Imperial) was a masonic ladies' night gift and is not connected with Judaism. Northwood made a similar design and other masonic items.*

This close-up of Double Dutch (Imperial) reveals a wooded coastal inlet more reminiscent of the Baltic than Holland. This design, produced by German immigrants, would have sold well to the multitudes who had migrated from the north of Europe. The mouldwork is extraordinary.

PRIME CARNIVAL GLASS
(USA, 1908-28)

At a trade show in the autumn of 1907, the newly founded Fenton Art Glass Company showed the first samples of 'a new iridescent glass called *Iridill* which has a metallic lustre much like the Tiffany favrile glass'. Frank Leslie Fenton and Jacob Rosenthal had simplified the once complicated and sometimes toxic coating process. Rosenthal was a clever glass technologist who had supervised production of the 'Chocolate' and the incomparable 'Holly Agate' types of pressed glass at the Greentown works of the Indiana Tumbler and Goblet Company before fire forced its closure. He settled with the Fenton family. Frank Leslie Fenton was responsible for the brilliant and eclectic designs, which, when iridised, both dazzled the eye and stimulated the imagination. The trade approved the designs and placed orders with the Fenton Company,

which ordered the mould blanks and tooling needed for mass production of the glass, which began in 1908.

The public loved the new glass and it sold on its own merits. The delighted purchasers did not notice that their dainty dishes were remarkably similar to the Tiffany product. Tiffany himself would have been embarrassed by the resemblance as he had little interest in selling to the masses. The processes of the art glass firms had been deliberately cloaked in mystery. There were hints of rediscovered oriental secrets, rare ingredients and exotic alchemy, all of which were well worth paying a high price for.

The market for expensive hand-made iridised glass collapsed as the demand for the new cheaper goods rose. The Fenton company originated prime Carnival and maintained its dominance as rival businesses took up the idea. Copying inevitably took place.

The Northwood Company was the first to market comparable glass. Harry Northwood was born in 1860 and left England to work in America in 1880. His father, John, was the most talented of the late Victorian glass manufacturers and the whole family was interested in glass. Harry liked the United States, perhaps because, although never losing touch with his family in England, he was out of the shadow of his father. In the course of a peripatetic but increasingly successful career he was variously employer and employee. Frank Leslie Fenton once worked for him.

Around 1900 the Northwood Company became part of the giant National Glass combine. Harry Northwood was in London for a while as the representative of this amalgam of many disparate American glass factories. He was thus in London in 1902 when his father died and he was an executor of his father's will, which excluded his half-brother John Northwood II. The latter inherited only the post of head designer at Stevens and Williams in his father's place. Frederick Carder, usurped *protégé* of Northwood senior, left England in high dudgeon and started afresh at Steuben in New York state. He maintained an ill concealed dislike for the Northwoods and anyone connected with them for the rest of his long life, even though it was Harry Northwood who had introduced Carder to his father in the first place.

Stevens and Williams and Webbs were only two of the Stourbridge firms that had iridised glass. Their techniques were taken to the United States by Harry Northwood and Frederick Carder. Tiffany's chief gaffer was Arthur Nash, who had learned his trade at Webbs. Not everyone in the iridescent glass business was English but the pivotal figure was Harry Northwood. When his factory produced iridised pressed glass in 1908 it was with little difficulty and it was no surprise. He sent a case of it, with other glass he had made, to his family in England to show his half-brother how their formulae and methods had been revived. Many years later John Northwood II maintained that it was his analysis of the original Fenton glass that had enabled Harry to reproduce it, but Harry

LEFT: *Pulled Loop flower vase (Fenton) with scalloped top. Pansy crimped oval dish (Imperial). Rib flower vase (Fenton) twisted round into a spiral helix with a fluted or flame edging.*
RIGHT: *Orange Tree (Fenton). In the foreground is a bowl (with Candy Ribbon crimp) and above it is a punch bowl with suspended cups, as sold. Note the adaptation of the design to suit each shape. The punch bowl stand is not shown.*

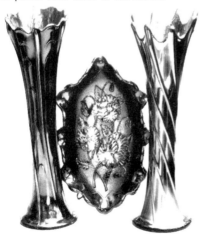

More Orange Tree items: a squat 'shaving' mug, a loving cup, a punch cup, a hatpin holder and another version of the mug shape, taller and narrower. Punch cups were sold separately in the United Kingdom for use with custard.

Northwood was a great and talented glassmaker in his own right.

Glass and Pottery World noted, in December 1908: 'The iridescent glass put out by Fenton and known to the manufacturers as *Rubi-glass* has been enjoying a great sale, especially in the ten cent stores. H. Northwood and Company have just produced a line almost identical in colour with the Fenton output. It will be called *Golden Iris.*' Both factories sold all the glass they could make but seemed unable to settle on consistent names for the new product. Parodies of the art glass trade names were used, to imply that for a small price the purchaser was buying instant culture. Typical advertisements offer Pompeian, Etruscan, Egyptian Iridescent, Rubi-gold, Helios, Venetian Art, Dragon-blue, Amberflame and Aurora Iris. Familiarity with classical language and art is apparent. The word Iris is from the Greek for rainbow and was much used.

In 1910 the Dugan Company, located in a factory previously worked by North-

wood, produced Carnival for the first time. Thomas Dugan was Harry Northwood's cousin on his mother's side, and they had worked together for a while. Dugan left his company in 1913 and, until the factory was destroyed by fire in 1931, the business traded as the Diamond Glass-ware Company, under which name most of its large output of iridescent glass was produced. Old Northwood moulds were used at this factory as well as exclusive Dugan designs and understandably it was thought that the firm was simply working under subcontract.

The Millersburg factory, at the eponymous town in Ohio, was founded by John Fenton, who, with his brother Robert, left the family company to start an independent works. A small amount of glass of the highest quality was produced before bankruptcy ended production under the Fentons. John Fenton had flamboyance but little business acumen and the company was foreclosed by the unpaid mouldmakers. Samuel Fair then bought and ran the works for a short

9

period as the Radium Glass Company. The factory produced from the spring of 1909 to June 1911 as Millersburg and for a few months from October 1911 as the Radium Glass Company. Carnival glass was made from early 1910 to closure.

The last major producer of prime Carnival was the Imperial Glass Company, reformed after insolvency as a corporation. Founded in 1901, it did not make iridised wares until 1910. It was a prolific factory specialising in moulded patterns based on brilliant cut glass. The rich and sophisticated 'triple doping' iridising process of Imperial resembles that on much Bohemian art glass of the period. Many German speaking workers from Bohemia were employed at the works in Bellaire, Ohio. It was not unusual for whole groups or workshops to emigrate en masse bringing their technical skills with them. The practice was eventually halted by the American trade unions. Metric tooling was used at the Imperial factory as the workmen had brought their own work kits with them. *Blow moulding* was a common Bohemian technique and there are some excellent blow-moulded pieces from Imperial.

Other American companies, both large and small, produced odd items or novelties in prime Carnival glass. Only the Westmoreland Glass Company and the United States Glass Company produced in a quantity worthy of note.

LEFT: *Designs from embroidery. Hearts and Flowers bowl (Northwood) with saw-tooth edge and gentle waved crimping. The flat plate in dark glass is Captive Rose pattern (Fenton).*
RIGHT: *Imperial vases for primroses, violets, sweet peas, carnations etc: Festoon, Morning Glory, Whalebone, Ripple and another example of Whalebone.*

Heavy Grape (Imperial). A close-up showing mouldmaking techniques. The alto relievo design is a result of drilled-out grapes, gouged stems and veining and a punched-in stippled background. This bravura pattern was enhanced with brilliant 'triple-doped' iridescence.

PRIME CARNIVAL DESIGNS

Although it became popular during the decline of Art Nouveau there is no trace of that movement in the designs of the prime Carnival output. The overwhelming influence is that of the Aesthetic movement of the 1880s. The peacock, which so fascinated the aesthetes, is to be found in both figurative and Japanese symbolic feather form. The convoluted and complicated patterns are filled out with petal forms and stippling. Other oriental motifs such as dragons, lotuses, butterflies and the ubiquitous chrysanthemum are to be found in startling juxtapositions and transformations that defy logic but delight the eye. There is much to amuse and divert. The Fenton design called 'Panther' shows an indeterminate feline looking very angry in a jungle of stylised peacock feathers. Rustic ele-

ments abound: twig feet, coral, bark, shells and petals were all used and the vine, in both foliate and fruit form, was a favourite. Many elements derive from the popular pressed glass patterns of a quarter of a century before. The nostalgia felt by immigrants for their homelands is manifested in patterns depicting windmills and tranquil fishing amidst banal Ruritanian backgrounds.

Flora, however, predominates, with occasional animals or birds appearing amid the undergrowth. The notions are quaint, exotic and naive in the same way that the silent films and romantic novels of the period are. Carnival reflects the popular culture of the period. It brought colour into drab homes and delighted a whole generation.

Some of the designs created for specific

use with an iridescent surface inspired magnificently executed glass moulds that have seldom been equalled. Designs inspired by delicate embroidery such as Hearts and Flowers, Captive Rose and Persian Medallion, show daring use of glass textures to imitate a rich satin stitch, enhanced by the matt lustre used on these patterns.

Other designs successfully recall *repoussé* metalwork. Bold textured designs, such as Heavy Grape, in combination with multicoloured iridescence produced effects that had never been seen before, nor have been since, on mass-produced glass.

A close study of the prime Carnival patterns, transmuted into glass by means of cast iron moulds, fills one with admiration for the artisans who chipped, drilled, filed and honed hard brittle metal into such delicate and intricate designs and shapes. The English emigrant family firm of Hipkins supplied very high quality moulds often offering variants of the same design to different companies. Noble but anonymous teams sweated over furnaces, heaved at hand presses, re-shaped, iridised and rushed glass around the factory. It still astonishes to find glass which received so much individual attention and so much handwork being sold for pennies.

BELOW: *Two ferneries sold originally with tin liners to protect the surface of the glass from the small plant pots and water: Vintage (Fenton) and Lustre Rose (Imperial). The Fenton item was also offered (without liner) as a nut bowl.*
BOTTOM: *Fruit or berry sets consisted of one large master bowl and six smaller ones. The difference in size can be seen here and the scarcity of the large bowls is simply due to the ratio of production. The pattern is Butterfly and Berry (Fenton).*

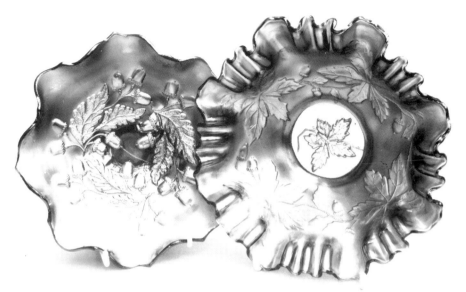

Two Fenton patterns that are often confused: Acorns on the left and Autumn Acorns on the right. The former has a scalloped edge with gentle crimps and the latter has Fenton's Candy Ribbon speciality crimping. The Acorns mould was beautifully made and designed.

COLOURS IN PRIME CARNIVAL

The colours used in Carnival production, in both the base glass and the metallic coating, are numerous and new combinations and variations are constantly being found. Selenium orange on clear base glass was the most popular colour. This is called *marigold* by collectors and exists in many varied tints and densities from pale gold to fiery orange-red coatings. It can be matt or mirror-like. Selenium is a rare element, discovered in 1817, which was found to give a brilliant orange as a colourant in pottery glazes, and in combination with the necessary stannous and ferrous chlorides it was used to produce 'golden' iridescence by the glass trade. It was used by Webbs for their *Iris* glass and also by Stevens and Williams long before its use as Carnival marigold. Red and green highlights can be found in a nominal marigold finish and were produced either inadvertently by impurities or deliberately by the use of small quantities of nitrates of strontium and barium. A rich very red semi-opaque marigold

contains cadmium sulphide. Marigold iridescence could be applied to glass of different colours so that varying effects would result.

The thinner the layer of metallic oxide is, then the more brilliant is the effect from the refraction of colour in the base glass. All metals combine with chlorine and the resulting chlorides are all soluble in water or alcohol mixtures. Different metals give different colours. The glass technologist had a full range of colours available in a fine droplet spray which does not crack hot glass. Reheating briefly is enough to produce a stable and saturated surface. There was little price difference between sprays of the various colours used. Marigold and its variations were the best sellers.

Some Carnival, as was Webbs' *Bronze*, was made by the old method of exposing the glass in a muffle to the fumes from chemicals burning in trays of charcoal in the bottom of the oven. In this method also stannous chloride was used. The idea

13

ABOVE: *Three easily found pot-boilers from Dugan: Windflower, Double Stem Roses and Cosmos Variant. These were made in large quantities in deteriorating moulds. Good crisp early mouldings are shown here. The two patterns to the right were the cheapest items of Carnival sold in Britain. They were on offer for 4d compared with the 6d to 9d charged for other bowls.*

BELOW: *Four rusticana vases that are similar enough to cause confusion. The dumpy April Showers vase (Fenton) has a shot silk version of Peacock Tail pattern inside. The Rustic and Hobnail vases, both by Fenton, are similar in theory but distinctly different in practice. The Treetrunk vase (Northwood) appears to be covered with tadpoles rather than bark.*

A Roseshow bowl (Northwood) flanked by a pair of Wreath of Roses rose or violet bowls (Dugan). The nut bowl in the centre was shaped from the standard Wreath of Roses shape shown. The depth of the mouldwork in the Northwood bowl is astonishing and reflects the skill of the hand-press operatives.

of its use came from mirror manufacturing, where the silver layer was not stable without it. It was noticed that incorrect temperatures for silvering produced unwanted rainbow iridescence. This side effect was used when the fashion for iridescent glass began.

Purple glass, from the deepest black violet to pastel amethyst, was very popular and spectacular iridescence of great intensity and depth is possible on this rich colour. The tints of the surface lustre can be deceptive and the base colour of the glass can often be seen only when it is held up to the light. The very dark purple appears black.

All shades of blue were produced and a consistently excellent cobalt glass of very rich blue was made by both Fenton and Northwood. Blue compounds applied to cobalt pressings give a splendid effect, especially on the peacock patterns. Northwood had a special shivering blue formula which much resembles the startling iridescence of tropical butterfly wings.

Green was also popular and ranges from a dark bottle green through to pastel olive and lime shades of great subtlety.

These were the staple colours of prime Carnival. Smaller quantities were made in amber, grey-blue, smoke, frosted semi-opaque white, pale acid-green vaseline and true traffic-signal red. Opalescent edgings or highlights, mainly by the Northwood and Dugan-Diamond works, were contrived by reheating cooling glass at a 'glory hole' in the furnace. The semi-opaque milkiness of the opalescent Carnival from these two factories extends from the edge and shades well towards the centre of the piece. Fenton made such glass but reheated using a gas jet under which the item was turned. This produced a finer, narrower band of opalescence. White milk glass and pale ivory custard glass were also iridised but produced a dull lack-lustre effect due to the loss of refraction in the opaque base glass.

Specimens of red or shaded red to amber *amberina* Carnival are scarce. The selenium-ruby formula used for red glass of this period was not developed for pressed goods until the mid 1920s, when demand for prime Carnival was falling. Most red was made by Fenton, with some from Imperial.

Fenton was the pioneer and developer of Carnival and produced more patterns, more shapes and more unusual varieties than any other company. Next by volume is Northwood, followed closely by Imperial, and then by Dugan-Diamond. Of the five largest producers of prime Carnival Millersburg made the least. The combined output of Westmoreland and United States Glass equals that of Millersburg.

BELOW: *Two pieces from the same mould which have different collectors' names. The Raspberry tripod dish (Northwood) on the left has the same pattern as that concealed within the Daisy and Plume rose bowl on the right.*
BOTTOM: *Two loving cup shaped ornaments: Orange Tree (Fenton) and Mary Ann (Dugan). The former has a Peacock Tail interior design and the latter exists in a three-handled version.*

Punch bowl and stand in Memphis (Northwood). The two punch cups are Fashion (Imperial) and Peacock-at-the-Fountain (Northwood). Customers in the United States were offered this bowl for fruit and a larger one for punch, both of which fitted into a common stand.

PRIME CARNIVAL SHAPES

Carnival glass was made in most of the shapes that are feasible in moulded glass but the bowl, in every possible variation, was the mainstay of the trade. Theoretical uses have been assigned to various configurations but the glass was so decorative that most pieces have not been used. Old company catalogues show the intended use for each shape, often contradicting later assumptions. Some pieces of prime Carnival are still in such pristine condition that it is difficult to believe they are old.

The quickest shape to press is a shallow bowl. This can easily be pushed down into a flat plate or pulled up into a deep bowl. Some bowls started as flat plates. However, all the prime Carnival makers were determined to individualise each piece. Being art glass, albeit mass-produced, it was crimped, pleated, pulled and swung into delightful variations. Only on the now scarce plain flat plates and uncrimped bowls can the patterns be seen in undistorted form.

The makers made sure that as little as possible left the works in the form in which it was moulded. Vases were taken when hot and swung round until elongated by centrifugal force. The edge of the open top was then crimped or formed into elegant ellipses. Whimsical variations were regular production items. Goblets were shaped into comports, rose bowls into candy dishes and vice versa. The workers produced coat-pocket friggers, beloved of all glassmen, and tumblers were transformed into vases or cuspidors. Items of this nature are now a collector's delight. There were table, punch, water and wine sets. Patterns were adapted for use on a variety of shapes, the 'Grape and Cable' design by Northwood being available on more items than any other.

17

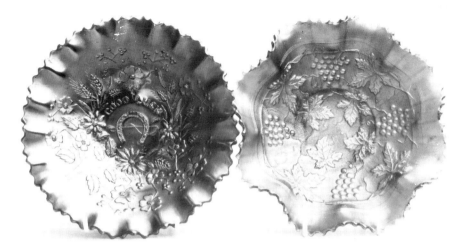

ABOVE: *Two best-selling bowls from Northwood. The motto-ware Good Luck was suitable for any occasion and there is a Fenton bowl with this wording but a different design. The other bowl is a Grape and Cable example from the most extensive range of items ever made in one design in Carnival.*

BELOW: *Three elegant comports from Fenton, Iris and Persian Medallion at the back and the smaller one at the front, Holly pattern. All have different stems and crimping but have the non-iridisation of the foot and stem in common.*

18

ABOVE: *Two handled bon-bon dishes by Fenton. The Wreath of Roses example has a stem whilst the Birds and Cherries is on a simple collar base. Note the different shaping. Dugan made a rose bowl in Wreath of Roses design that differs from the Fenton version.*

BELOW: *Three splendid plates from Northwood: Three Fruits, Strawberry and Wishbone. The last design is of orchids. Northwood was the only maker of prime Carnival to mark his goods but not all of them will be found with the trademark of an N underlined.*

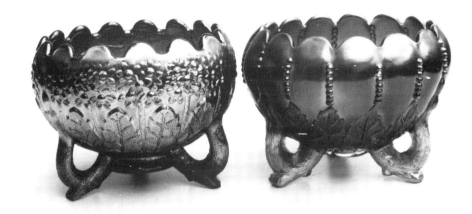

ABOVE: *Plagiarism was frequent amongst glass manufacturers and here are two nut bowls in the same configuration from Fenton and Northwood. The patterns are different, however: Orange Tree, and Leaf and Beads. The identical rustic twig feet are charming. These are collected as rose bowls.*

BELOW: *Sailboats and Little Fishes, two Fenton designs of great quaintness and charm.*

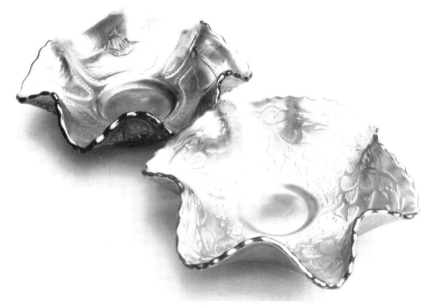

ABOVE: *Fern (Northwood) and Cherries (Dugan), two excellent examples of very reflective brilliant iridescence. Cherries was long thought to be a Northwood pattern and can still be found listed as such.*

BELOW: *The Peacocks bowl (Northwood) on the left has a pie-crust crimp whilst the Peacock and Urn bowl (Fenton) on the right is gently waved. The interior of a Fenton comport is shown in the centre. Millersburg, Northwood and, it is thought, Dugan all made versions of the Peacock and Urn design.*

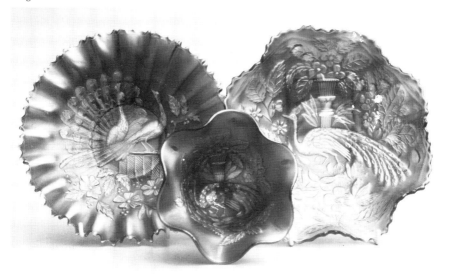

ABOVE: *Tumblers in Panelled Dandelion (Fenton), Diamond Lace (Imperial) and Floral and Grape (Fenton). Dugan copied Floral and Grape very successfully.*

BELOW: *Wine sets from the Imperial factory: Octagon and Imperial Grape. Both decanters and both stoppers are blow-moulded whilst the matching stemmed glasses are press-moulded. Prime Imperial Carnival is not marked.*

22

ABOVE: *Tumblers by Northwood: Wishbone, Peacock-at-the-Fountain and Acorn Burrs, all in dark glass with rich, scintillating iridescence.*

BELOW: *Three pitchers of different capacities: Scale Band (Fenton), Windmill (Imperial), and Octagon (Imperial). The tumblers are Field Thistle (US Glass) and to the right Butterfly and Berry (Fenton).*

ABOVE: *A six-sided bowl in Heart and Vine pattern (Fenton), which depicts stylised peacock feathers. The handled bon-bon dish in the centre is Peacock Tail (Fenton) and Nippon (Northwood) is at the right. All these are peacock inspired and Nippon is taken from a Japanese design book.*

BELOW: *Peacock and Grape, and Dragon and Lotus. These were Fenton's staple patterns and were made and sold in vast quantities. The flat plate shapes are scarce.*

24

ABOVE: *A surprisingly simple and classic design. A small sugar and creamer in Cairo design by Westmoreland. These were advertised originally as being 'Egyptian Iridescent' goods.*

BELOW: *An assortment from a Butler Brothers wholesale catalogue. All the items are by Fenton, which, like other factories, packaged glass in barrel assortments for Butlers, who reshipped the casks unopened. Once the origin of one item is known, from a factory catalogue, then a whole assortment is identified.*

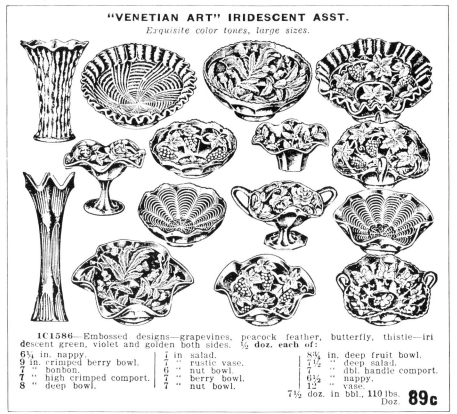

"VENETIAN ART" IRIDESCENT ASST.

Exquisite color tones, large sizes.

1C1586—Embossed designs—grapevines, peacock feather, butterfly, thistle—iridescent green, violet and golden both sides. ½ **doz. each of:**

6¼ in. nappy.	7 in. salad.	8¾ in. deep fruit bowl.
9 in. crimped berry bowl.	7 " rustic vase.	7½ " deep salad.
7 " bonbon.	6 " nut bowl.	7 " dbl. handle comport.
7 " high crimped comport.	7 " berry bowl.	6½ " nappy.
8 " deep bowl.	7 " nut bowl.	12 " vase.

7½ doz. in bbl., 110 lbs.
Doz. **89c**

ABOVE: *Secondary Carnival Glass by Sowerby. The Wickerwork dish with stand, the Daisyblock flower boat and the four-handled dish are all from salvaged, late nineteenth-century moulds. The boat had its plain interior replaced by a new ribbed design. The formerly plain small dish had a 'new' Scroll Embossed interior added which was copied from an Imperial design.*

BELOW: *Sowerby made the Swan butterdish from an old mould. A later version filled in the open neck space. Sowerby also produced the 'Chic' hen from a mould bought in during the 1920s as well as the black, plain panelled Gateshead candlestick. The taller Moonprint candlestick was made in Germany by Brockwitz.*

Secondary Carnival made in Holland. A celery vase, Fine Cut Rings, and a stemmed sugar, Rembrandt, both made at the Royal Leerdam works in the late 1920s. The celery vase is an English registered design of M. Guggenheim and Company of London and was made by Leerdam to order. Rembrandt is an old original Leerdam mould.

SECONDARY CARNIVAL GLASS (AUSTRALIA AND EUROPE, 1920-39)

Demand for prime Carnival fell in the United States as mechanisation spread. Glass was made by the continuous tank method and shaped by machine pressing, and so vast quantities of simple, cheap glass became available for everyday use. Standards of hygiene improved, the decor of even the humblest home was streamlined and popular culture became more sophisticated. Even so, the popularity of Carnival lasted longer outside the United States where change was slower.

The first Carnival to be made outside the United States was the glass made in Australia. Crystal Glass Ltd registered many Australian designs as trade marks as well as the usual registered designs. This was because they did not want to have the glass marked with ugly numbers. This Carnival is probably the best glass made in Australia and was issued initially to compete with the American import. It then replaced it. The glass was not exported commercially. It is of good quality and the designs of Australian flora and fauna are delightful. Cristalerias Piccardo in Argentina produced marigold items including water and wine sets, table items, vases and decorative dishes during the 1930s.

The Australian Carnival was the only secondary glass to rival the American. The Carnival produced in Europe was made to supply the demand that still existed as the American product was phased out. Prime Carnival was copied as well as each firm was able. In England the only documented producer was Sowerby's Ellison Glassworks at Gateshead. Here moulds were revived that in some cases dated from the 1880s. Some new interior plungers were made with iridescence in mind. They were taken from Imperial pattern books and have caused much confusion. Sowerby Carnival, like the secondary products from elsewhere, was limited in colour to

27

ABOVE: *The Brockwitz factory, near Meissen in Saxony, produced the extensive Curved Star range of goods. Although made in a variety of colours, these were only iridised by Brockwitz in marigold and in blue. Many moulds supplied by this large works were used elsewhere in Germany, Czechoslovakia, Scandinavia and Argentina.*

LEFT: *The massive epergne in Curved Star by Brockwitz is in three parts fastened by a metal screw and socket cemented into the upper and lower parts. It is part of the extensive table ware service in this pattern. A pair of celery vases is also shown; these were called 'chalices' by early collectors. The moulded raspberry prunts recall traditional Central European glass decoration.*

a simple selenium spray on clear glass and a darker coating on blue or amethyst glass. The former was referred to as *Sunglow* and the latter as *Rainbo Lustre*. This glass was exported widely throughout the British Empire from 1926 to 1930. Unsold stocks remained in the cellars and attics of Sowerby's works until long after the Second World War. The peacock head trademark can be found on some but not all Sowerby-made Carnival. This Gateshead-made glass has been found in India, Singapore, South Africa, Zimbabwe, Zambia, Australia and New Zealand. It reached the United States through bulk antique consignments from the mid 1960s onwards.

However, the largest manufacturer of all during the secondary period was Brockwitz in Germany. This factory produced consistent, uniformly iridised and well finished goods throughout the 1930s. The firm specialised in extensive suites of goods of many matching items. Curved Star was their most popular range with the simpler Moonprint and Triands patterns following closely behind. Their rich marigold has a mirror-like finish and the deep rich lustre on their blue glass is consistent. Brockwitz produced in quantity at reasonable prices and sold their moulded glassware throughout Europe. The catalogues of this firm display an extensive repertoire of stylistically consistent patterns and shapes indicative of a huge metal mould workshop and store. The business also had an impressive archive of well maintained old moulds which they revived in the 1930s. Moulds made by Brockwitz found their way to other factories particularly in Scandinavia. In Finland Riihimäen Lasi Oy had a small range of high quality iridised goods. In Sweden the Eda glassworks produced a small amount of Carnival. With the exception of the cheap marigold jobbing items from Karhula-Iitala, Scandinavian patterns enjoyed only a very limited circulation.

Carnival jewellery and novelties such as blow-moulded Christmas tree ornaments, hatpins and buttons were made in the Gablonz (Jablonec) region of Czechoslovakia. This area still specialises in making small decorative items of fashion glass.

Jewellery made at Gablonz (Jablonec) in Czechoslovakia. The rosary is marked 'Lourdes' and must have been sold there.

New Carnival. The bell, the cat paperweight and the Peacock vase are by Fenton and are marked, as all the firm's new glass is, with a script 'Fenton' in an oval cartouche. The unmarked hen was made by the Indiana Glass Company and the shoe was made by the Smith Glass Company and is marked SGC. Many UK and Australian collectors regularly import selections of American-made new Carnival. It is mostly sentimental kitsch, far removed from the dignified original.

COLLECTING CARNIVAL GLASS

Iridescent glass remained unseen, unwanted and forgotten for several generations. The original logical sequence of production was not known. Records were lost. Astute glass collectors were able to buy iridescent glass of all types for paltry sums. Tiffany glass was the first to be rehabilitated, then the Bohemian output.

Carnival collecting has been well organised in the United States since the early 1960s but its rehabilitation is static. Academic progress is generally ignored. The export of antiques from Europe to the USA in containers was a boom industry from about 1965 until 1978, and in this way tea chests full of unsorted Carnival reached North America. The original prime Carnival was mixed up with European secondary and both were offered for sale by American antique dealers, together with any other moulded glass that had been given an iridescent spray.

The pioneer collectors of Carnival thus had a difficult task, which was made even harder when new and reproduction Carnival began to be made as a result of their interest. Factory catalogues and archives were not yet to hand and elaborate guesswork was responsible for confusing factory attributions that have subsequently had to be corrected. Much of the literature on the subject, although honestly and painstakingly written, is misleading. Nevertheless all research must start from these books and without them the continual piecing together of the Carnival production sequence would not have been possible. There has been some confusion over pattern names but luckily succinct names have become generally accepted and clumsy ones discarded.

Any collector of Carnival glass needs the help and advice of fellow enthusiasts, especially in distinguishing new and reproduction pieces. Membership of the Carnival Glass Society (UK), founded in 1982, is strongly recommended.

BIBLIOGRAPHY

Amaya, Mario. *Tiffany Glass*. Studio Vista, 1967.

Archer, Margaret and Douglas. *Imperial Glass*. Collector Books, USA, 1978. Valuable catalogue reprints.

Arwas, Victor. *Glass, Art Nouveau to Art Deco*. Academy Editions, 1977.

Australian Carnival Glass Enthusiasts Inc. *Carnival Glass of Australia*. ACE, Australia, 1989. The most reliable guide to Australian Carnival glass.

Baker, Gary E.; Eige, G. Eason; McCluskey, Holly Hoover; Measell, James S.; Spillman, Jane Shadel; and Wilson, Kenneth M. *Wheeling Glass – 1829-1939*. Oglebay Institute Glass Museum, USA, 1994. Excellent museum catalogue with full coverage of Northwood.

Cosentino, G., and Stewart, R. *Carnival Glass*. Golden Press, USA, 1976.

Dodsworth, Roger. *Glass and Glassmaking*. Shire Publications, 1982; reprinted 1993. A good basic guide to glass.

Edwards, Bill. *The Standard Encyclopedia of Carnival Glass*. Collector Books, USA, 1985. A compilation of comments on assorted pictures supplied by collectors.

Florence, Gene. *Depression Glass*. Collector Books, USA, 1979. This is the machine-made glass that ousted Carnival.

Fox, Dorothea M. 'Tiffany Glass'. *Antiques Magazine* (USA), XLIV (1943) 240-1, 295-6. This was the beginning of the rehabilitation of Tiffany.

Freeman, Larry. *Iridescent Glass*. Century House, USA, 1956. The first book on the subject.

Gardner, Paul V. *The Glass of Frederick Carder*. Crown Publishers, USA, 1976.

Garner, Philippe (editor). *Phaidon Encyclopedia of Decorative Arts 1890-1940*. Phaidon, 1978.

Graham, Marjorie. *Australian Glass*. David Ell Press, 1981. Covers Australian Carnival production.

Hartung, Marion. *Carnival Glass in Color*. Privately printed, USA, 1967.

— *Northwood Pattern Glass in Color*. Privately printed, USA, 1967.

— *Carnival Glass Patterns*. Ten volumes, privately printed, USA. Most names for Carnival pieces come from these books.

Heacock, William. 'Carnival Glass by the United States Glass Company'. *Glass Collector* (USA), Spring 1982, 3-5.

— *Fenton Glass, The First Twenty-five Years*. O-Val Advertising Corporation, USA, 1978 and subsequent editions.

— *Fenton Glass, The Second Twenty-five Years*. O-Val Advertising Corporation, USA, 1980.

— *Fenton Glass, The Third Twenty-five Years*. O-Val Advertising Corporation, USA, 1990.

— *Harry Northwood – The Early Years 1881-1900*. Antique Publications, USA, undated.

— *Harry Northwood – The Wheeling Years 1901-1925*. Antique Publications, USA, 1991. These two excellent books are the definitive history of the Northwood company.

— *Opalescent Glass from A-Z*. Antique Publications, USA, 1977.

— *US Glass from A-Z*. Antique Publications, USA, 1978.

Heacock, William; Measell, James; and Wiggins, Berry. *Dugan/Diamond – The Story of Indiana, Pennsylvania, Glass*. Antique Publications, USA, 1993. A scholarly and definitive history.

Janson, S.E. *Glass Technology*. HMSO, 1969.

Jenning's Design Company (Publisher). *A Catalog Reprint of Dugan Glass Company and H. Northwood Co., Glass Manufacturers*. USA, undated. A reprint of the only known trade catalogues of these two companies.

Koch, Robert. *Louis C. Tiffany, Rebel in Glass*. Crown Publishers, USA, 1964.

— *Louis C. Tiffany's Glass, Bronzes, Lamps*. Crown Publishers, USA, 1975.

— *Louis C. Tiffany's Art Glass*. Crown Publishers, USA, 1978.

Manley, Cyril. *Decorative Victorian Glass*. Ward Lock, 1981.

— 'English Iridescent Glass'. *Spinning Wheel* (USA), January/February 1969, 14-16, 54. An

important early article.
— 'The Irresolute Progress of Iridescent Glass'. CGS Journal, winter 1982, 2-4.
Measell, James. *Greentown Glass*. Grand Rapids Public Museum, USA, 1979. The early career of Jacob Rosenthal.
Moore, Donald. *The Shape of Things in Carnival Glass*. Privately printed, USA, undated. An excellent standard exposition.
— *Carnival Glass Rarities*. Privately printed, USA, 1982. Specialised but very accurate.
Notley, Raymond. 'Sowerby Carnival Glass'. Glass Collector (USA), spring 1982, 26-9.
— 'Sowerby Carnival Patterns'. *HOACGA Bulletin* (USA), twenty-four articles, monthly, 1982-3.
— *Journal of the Carnival Glass Society*, 1-14, 1983-8.
— *Poor Man's Tiffany*. Castle Museum, Nottingham, 1983. Exhibition catalogue with two essays and notes.
— 'The Unknown Northwood'. *The Glass Cone*, number 2, June 1984. New material concerning Harry Northwood.
Owens, Richard E. *Carnival Glass Tumblers*. Wallace Homestead Book Company, USA, 1978.
Revi, A. C. *American Art Nouveau Glass*. Schiffer, USA, 1968.
— *Nineteenth Century Glass*. Galahad Books, USA, 1967.
Scholes, Samuel R. 'The American Table Ware Industry'. *Pottery Gazette*, 1916, 745-7, 835-7.
Spillman, Jane Shadel. *American and European Pressed Glass Catalogue*. Corning Museum of Glass, USA, 1981.
Thompson, Jenny. *The Identification of English Pressed Glass*. Nunwick Hall, Penrith, 1989.
Turner, W. S. 'The Glass Industry in North America'. *Pottery Gazette*, 1920, 927-30.
Umbraco, K. and R. *Iridescent Stretch Glass*. Privately printed, USA, 1972.
Weatherman, Hazel Marie. *Colored Glassware of the Depression Era* (2 volumes). Glassbooks, USA, 1970, 1974.
Weissberger, Herbert. 'After Many Years. Tiffany Glass'. *Carnegie Magazine* (USA) 30, October 1956, 256-68.
Zsigmondy, Richard. 'Metallic-Lustre on Ceramics and Glass'. *Pottery Gazette*, 1904, 976.
— 'Iridescent Glass Recipes'. *Pottery Gazette*, 1927, 131.
— 'Lustred Pottery. Ancient and Modern'. *Pottery Gazette*, 1923, 95-7.
Bound volumes of the following trade journals contain much relevant information: *The Pottery Gazette, Glass, Pottery and Glass Record, National Glass Budget, Glass Pottery Review, Die Glashütte* (Dresden), *Le Verre, Journal du Ceramiste du Chaufournier*.

USEFUL INFORMATION
Broadfield House Glass Museum, Barnett Lane, Kingswinford, West Midlands DY6 9QA. Telephone: 01384 273011. The Notley-Lerpiniere Collection of a thousand items is on permanent loan. Displays are regularly changed and items not on display can be seen by prior written appointment.
The only large reference collection is in Britain at the Broadfield House Glass Museum. In the United States Fenton maintains a magnificent company museum and their factory can be toured.
The Carnival Glass Society (UK) can be contacted c/o Broadfield House Glass Museum. Members receive reference material and regular pattern and news letters. There are regular auctions of Carnival glass in the USA. These and other private sales are advertised in the subscription weekly *Antique Trader*, PO Box 1050, Dubuque, Iowa 52001, USA.